My God, My Alphabet, and Myself!

Emi Seri

ISBN 979-8-88540-363-4 (paperback)
ISBN 979-8-88540-364-1 (digital)

Christian Faith Publishing
832 Park Avenue
Meadville, PA 16335
www.christianfaithpublishing.com

Printed in the United States of America

I dedicate this children's book to the following:

- The children the Lord has entrusted me with: Samuel Ralphian and Abigaelle-Lis Loyal
- My husband, Yannick Seri, the head of our household, as ordained by the Lord
- The church I attend and its pastor: Dr. Moussa Toure

A
B
A: God is awesome.

B: God is my beautifier.

C: God is my companion.

D: God is my deliverer.

E: God is excellent.

F: God is my father.

G: God is good.

H: God is my helper.

I: God is invincible.

J: God is just.

K: God is my keeper.

L: God is love.

M: God is magnificent.

N: God is my night watcher.

O: God is omnipotent, omniscient, and omnipresent.

P: God is praiseworthy.

16

Q: God is my quickener.

R: God is my rewarder.

17

Q

R

S: God is sovereign.

T: God is trustworthy.

U
V

U: God is unlimited.
V: God is victorious.

W: God is wonderful.
X: God is extraordinary.

Y: God yearns for me.
Z: God is zealous.

About the Author

Emi Seri is a firm believer in Jesus Christ, the Lord and Savior of humanity. Since receiving Jesus Christ as her personal Lord and Savior in February 2019, she has been growing in her faith, seeking and creating opportunities to live by it and live it out.

Traditionally, children's book is filled with lots of animals, fruits, and vegetables. Yes, it is important for our children to grow knowing the alphabet, animals, fruits, and vegetables. However, how much more important and beneficial would it be for our children to learn and know their Creator, Source, Father, and His character and attributes?

Whether you decide to use this book as a bedtime book or otherwise, let's be intentional in nurturing intellectual yet God-fearing and bold children.